MW00569889

The Battle Fought Between The Ancient And Modern Books In St. James' Library

Jonathan Swift

A FULL AND TRUE ACCOUNT
OF
THE BATTLE FOUGHT LAST FRIDAY
BETWEEN THE ANCIENT AND THE MODERN
BOOKS
IN SAINT JAMES'S LIBRARY.

The bookseller to the reader.

THE following discourse, as it is unquestionably of the same author, so it seems to have been written about the same time, with the former; I mean the year 1697, when the famous dispute was on foot about ancient and modern learning, The controversy took its rise from an essay of Sir William Temple's upon that subject; which was answered by W. Wotton, B.D., with an appendix by Dr. Bentley, endeavouring to destroy the credit of Æsop and Phalaris for authors, whom Sir William Temple had, in the before mentioned, highly commended. In that appendix the doctor falls hard upon a new edition of Phalaris, put out by the Honourable Charles Boyle, now Earl of Orrery, to which Mr. Boyle replied at large with great learning and wit; and the doctor voluminously rejoined. In this dispute the town highly resented to see a person of Sir William Temple's character and merits roughly used by the two reverend gentlemen aforesaid, and without any manner of provocation. At length, there appearing no end of the quarrel, our author tells us that the BOOKS in St. James's Library, looking upon themselves as parties principally concerned, took up the controversy, and came to a decisive battle; but the manuscript, by the injury of fortune or weather, being in several places imperfect, we cannot learn to which side the victory fell.

I must warn the reader to beware of applying to persons what is here meant only of books, in the literal sense. So, when Virgil is mentioned, we are not to understand the person of a famous poet called by that name; but only certain sheets paper of bound up in leather, containing in print the works of the said poet: and so of the rest.

The preface of the author.

Satire is a sort of glass wherein beholders do generally discover everybody's face but their own; which is the chief reason for that kind reception it meets with in the world, and that so very few are offended with it. But, if it should happen otherwise, the danger is not great; and I have learned from long experience never to apprehend mischief from those understandings I have been able to provoke: for anger and fury, though they add strength to the sinews of the body, yet are found to relax those of the mind, and to render all its efforts feeble and impotent.

There is a brain that will endure but one scumming; let the owner gather it with discretion, and manage his little stock with husbandry; but, of all things, let him beware of bringing it under the lash of his betters, because that will make it all bubble up into impertinence, and he will find no new supply. Wit without knowledge being a sort of cream, which gathers in a night to the top, and by a skilful hand may be soon whipped into froth; but once scummed away, what appears underneath will be fit for nothing but to be thrown to the hogs.

THE BATTLE OF THE BOOKS.

Whoever examines, with due circumspection, into the annual records of time, will find it remarked that war is the child of pride, and pride the daughter of riches:— the former of which assertions may be soon granted, but one cannot so easily subscribe to the latter; for pride is nearly related to beggary and want, either by father or mother, and sometimes by both: and to speak naturally, it very seldom happens among men to fall out when all have enough; invasions usually travelling from north to south thas is to say, from poverty to plenty. The most ancient and natural grounds of quarrels are lust and avarice; which, though we may allow to be brethren, or collateral branches of pride, are certainly the issues of want. For, to speak in the phrase of writers upon politics, we may observe in the republic of dogs, which in its original seems to be an institution of the many, that the whole state is ever in the profoundest peace after a full meal; and that civil broils arise among them when it happens for one great bone to be seized on by some leading dog, who either divides it among the few, and then it falls to an oligarchy, or keeps it to himself, and then it ruus up to a tyranny. The same reasoning also holds place among them in those dissensions we behold upon a turgescency in any of their females. For the right of possession lying in common (it being impossible to establish a property in so delicate a case), jealousies and suspicions do so abound, that the whole commonwealth of that street is reduced to a manifest state of war, of every citizen against every citizen, till some one of more courage, conduct. or fortune than the rest seizes and enjoys the price: upon which naturally arises plenty of heart-burning, and envy, and snarling against the happy dog. Again, if we look upon any of these republics engaged in a foreign war, either of invasion or defence, we shall find the same reasoning will serve as to the grounds and occasions of each; and that poverty or want, in some degree or other (whether real or in opinion, which makes no alteration in the case), has a great share, as well as pride, on the part of the aggressor.

Now, whoever will please to take this scheme, and either reduce or adapt it to an intellectual state or commonwealth of learning, will soon discover the first ground of disagreement between the two great parties at this time in arms, and may form just conclusions upon the merits of either cause. But the issue or events of this war are not so easy to conjecture at; for the present quarrel is so inflamed by the warm heads of either faction, and the pretensions somewhere or other so exorbitant, as not to admit the least overtures of accommodation. This quarrel first began, as I have heard it affirmed by an old dweller in the neighbourhood, about a small spot of ground, lying and being upon one of the two tops of the hill Parnassus; the highest and largest of which had, it seems, been time out of mind in quiet possession of certain tenants, called the Ancients; and the other was held by the Moderns. But these, disliking their present station, sent certain ambassadors to the ancients, complaining of a great nuisance; how the height of that part of Parnassus quite spoiled the prospect of theirs, especially toward the *east;* and therefore, to avoid a war, offered them the choice of this alternative, either that the ancients would please to remove themselves and their effects down to the lower summit, which the moderns would graciously surrender to them, and advance into their place; or else the said ancients will give leave to the moderns to come with shovels and mattocks, and level the said hill as low as they shall think it convenient. To which the ancients made answer, how little they expected such a message as this from a colony whom they had admitted, out of their own free grace, to so near a neighbourhood. That, as to their own seat, they were aborigines of it, and therefore to talk with them of a removal or surrender was a language they did not understand. That if the height of the hill on their side shortened the prospect of the moderns, it was a disadvantage they could not help; but desired them to consider whether that injury (if it be any) were not largely recompensed by the shade and shelter it afforded them. That as to the levelling or digging down, it was either folly or ignorance to propose it if they did or did not know how that side of the hill was an entire rock, which would break their tools and hearts, without any damage to itself. That they would therefore advise the moderns rather to raise their own side of the hill than dream of pulling down that of the ancients; to the former of which they would not only give licence, but also largely contribute. All this was rejected by the moderns with much indignation, who still insisted upon one of the two expedients; and so this difference broke out into a long and obstinate war, maintained on the one part by resolution, and by the courage of certain leader and allies; but, on the other, by the greatness of their number, upon all defeats affording continual recruits. In this quarrel whole rivulets of ink have been exhausted, and the virulence of both parties enormously augmented. Now, it must be here understood that ink is the great missive weapon in all battles of the learned, which, conveyed through a sort of engine called a quill, infinite numbers of these are darted at the enemy by the valiant on each side, with equal skill and violence, as if it were an engagement of *porcupines*. This malignant liquor was compounded, by the engineer who invented it, of two ingredients, which are, gall and copperas; by its bitterness and venom to suit, in some degree, as well as to foment, the genius of the combatants. And as the Grecians, after an engagement, when they could not agree about the victory, were wont to set up trophies on both sides, the beaten party being content to be at the same expense, to keep itself in countenance (a laudable and ancient custom, happily revived of late in the art of war), so the learned, after a sharp and bloody dispute, do, on both sides, hang out their trophies too, whichever comes by the worst. These trophies have largely inscribed on them the merits of the cause; a full impartial account of such a *battle*, and how the victory fell clearly to the party that set them up. They are known to the world under several names;

159

as disputes, arguments, rejoinders, brief considerations answers, replies, remarks, reflections, objections, confutations. For a very few days they are fixed up in all public places, either by themselves or their representatives, for passengers to gaze at; whence the chiefest and largest are removed to certain magazines they call libraries, there to remain in a quarter purposely assigned them, and thenceforth begin to be called books of controversy.

In these books is wonderfully instilled and preserved the spirit of each warrior while he is alive; and after his death his soul transmigrates thither to inform them. This at least is the more common opinion; but I believe it is with libraries as with other cemeteries; where some philosophers affirm that a certain spirit, which they call *brutum hominis*, hovers over the monument, till the body is corrupted and turns to dust or to worms, but then vanishes or dissolves; so. we may say, a restless spirit haunts over every book, till dust or worms have seized upon it; which to some may happen in a few days, but to others later: and therefore books of controversy, being, of all others, haunted by the most disorderly spirits. have always been confined in a separate lodge from the rest; and for fear of a mutual violence against, each other. it was thought prudent by our ancestors to bind them to the peace with strong iron chains. Of which invention the original occasion was this: When the works of Scotus first came out. they were carried to a certain library, and had lodgings appointed them; but this author was no sooner settled than he went to visit his master, Aristotle; and there both concerted together to seize Plato by main force. and turn him out from his ancient station among the divines, where he had peaceably dwelt near eight hundred years. The attempt succeeded, and the two usurpers have reigned ever since in his stead; but, to maintain quiet for the future, it was decreed that all *polemics* of the larger size should be held fast with a chain.

By this expedient the public peace of libraries might certainly have been preserved if a new species of controversial books had not arisen of late years, instinct with a more malignant spirit, from the war above mentioned between the learned about the higher summit of *Parnassus*.

When these books were first admitted into the public libraries, I remember to have said, upon occasion, to several persons concerned, how I was sure they would create broils wherever they came, unless a world of care were taken: and therefore I advised that the champions of each side should be coupled together, or otherwise mixed, that, like the blending of contrary poisons, their malignity might be employed among themselves. And it seems I was neither an ill prophet nor an ill counsellor; for it was nothing else but the neglect of this caution which gave occasion to the terrible fight that happened on Friday last between the ancient and modern books in the king's library. Now, because the talk of this battle is so fresh in everybody's mouth, and the expectation of the town so great to be informed in the particulars, I, being, possessed of all qualifications requisite in an historian, and retained by neither party, have resolved to comply with the urgent importunity of my friends, by writing down a full impartial account thereof.

The guardian of the regal library*, a person of great valour, but chiefly renowned for his humanity, had been a fierce champion for the moderns; and, in an engagement upon Parnassus, had vowed, with his own hands to knock down two of the ancient chiefs, who guarded a small pass on the superior rock; but, endeavouring to climb up, was cruelly obstructed by his own unhappy weight and tendency towards his centre; a quality to which those of the modern

---

* The Honourable Mr. Boyle, in the preface to his edition of Phalaris, says he was refused a MS. by the royal librarian, Dr. Bentley.

party are extremely subject; for, being light-headed, they have, in speculation, a wonderful agility, and conceive nothing too high for them to mount; but, in reducing to practice, discover a mighty pressure about their posteriors and their heels. Having thus failed in his design, the disappointed champion bore a cruel rancour to the ancients; which he resolved to gratify by showing all marks of his favour to the books of their adversaries, and lodging them in the fairest apartments; when, at the same time, whatever book had the boldness to own itself for an advocate of the ancients was buried alive in some obscure corner, and threatened, upon the least displeasure, to be turned out of doors. Besides, it so happened that about this time there was a strange confusion of place among all the books in the library; for which several reasons were assigned. Some imputed it to a great heap of learned dust, which a perverse wind blew off from a shelf of moderns into the keeper's eyes. Others affirmed he had a humour to pick the worms out of the schoolmen, and swallow them fresh and fasting: whereof some fell upon his spleen, and some climbed up into his head, to the great perturbation of both. And lastly, others maintained that, by walking much in the dark about the library, he had quite lost the situation of it out his head; and therefore, in replacing his books, he was apt to mistake, and clap Des Cartes next to Aristotle; poor Plato had got between Hobbes and the Seven Wise Masters, and Virgil was hemmed in with Dryden on one side and Withers on the other.

Meanwhile those books that were advocates for the moderns chose out one from among them to make a progress through the whole library, examine the number and strength of their party, and concert their affairs. This messenger performed all things very industriously, and brought back with him a list of their forces, in all, fifty thousand, consisting chiefly of light-horse, heavy-armed foot, and mercenaries; whereof the foot were in general but sorrily armed and worse clad; their horses large. but extremely out of case and heart; however, some few, by trading among the ancients, had furnished themselves tolerably enough.

While things were in this ferment, discord grew extremely high; but words passed on both sides, and ill blood was plentifully bred. Here a solitary ancient, squeezed up among a whole shelf of moderns, offered fairly to dispute the case, and to prove by manifest reason that the priority was due to them from long possession, and in regard of their prudence, antiquity, and, above all, their great merits toward the moderns. But these denied the premises, and seemed very much to wonder how the ancients could pretend to insist upon their antiquity, when it was so plain (if they went to that) that the moderns were much the more ancient of the two. As for any obligations they owed to the ancients, they renounced them all. It is true, said they, we are informed some few of our party have been so mean to borrow their subsistence from you; but the rest, infinitely the greater number (and especially we French and English), were so far from stooping to so base an example, that there never passed, till this very hour, six words between us. For our horses were of our own breeding, our arms of our own forging, and our clothes of our own cutting out and sewing. Plato was by chance up on the next shelf, and observing those that spoke to be in the ragged plight mentioned a while ago; their jades lean and foundered, their weapons of rotten wood, their armour rusty, and nothing but rags underneath; he laughed loud, and in his pleasant way swore, by ——, he believed them.

Now, the moderns had not proceeded in their late negotiation with secrecy enough to escape the notice of the enemy. For those advocates who had begun the quarrel, by setting first on foot the dispute of precedency, talked so loud of coming to a battle, that Sir William Temple happened to overhear them, and gave immediate intelligence to the ancients:

who thereupon drew up their scattered troops together, resolving to act upon the defensive; upon which, several of the moderns fled over to their party, and among the rest Temple himself. This Temple, having been educated and long conversed among the ancients, was, of all the moderns, their greatest favourite, and became their greatest champion.

Things were at this crisis when a material accident fell out. For upon the highest corner of a large window there dwelt a certain spider, swollen up to the first magnitude by the destruction of infinite numbers of flies, whose spoils lay scattered before the gates of his palace, like human bones before the cave of some giant. The avenues to his castle were guarded with turnpikes and palisadoes, all after the modern way of fortification. After you had passed several courts you came to the centre, wherein you might behold the constable himself in his own lodgings, which had windows fronting to each avenue, and ports to sally out upon all occasions of prey or defence. In this mansion he had for some time dwelt in peace and plenty, without danger to his person by swallows from above, or to his palace by brooms from below; when it was the pleasure of fortune to conduct thither a wandering bee, to whose curiosity a broken pane in the glass had discovered itself, and in he went; where, expatiating a while, he at last happened to alight upon one of the outward walls of the spider's citadel; which, yielding to the unequal weight, sunk down to the very foundation. Thrice he endeavoured to force his passage, and thrice the centre shook. The spider within, feeling the terrible convulsion, supposed at first that nature was approaching to her final dissolution; or else, that Beelzebub, with all his legions, was come to revenge the death of many thousands of his subjects whom his enemy had slain and devoured. However, he at length valiantly resolved to issue forth and meet his fate. Meanwhile the bee had acquitted himself of his toils, and, posted securely at some distance, was employed in cleansing his wings, and disengaging them from the ragged remnants of the cobweb. By this time the spider was adventured out. when, beholding the chasms. the ruins, and dilapidations of his fortress, he was very near at his wits' end; he stormed and swore like a madman, and swelled till he was ready to burst. At length. casting his eye upon the bee. and wisely gathering causes from events (for they knew each other by sight): A plague split you, said he. for a giddy son of a whore; is it you, with a vengeance, that have made this litter here? could not you look before you, and be d——d? do you think I have nothing else to do (in the devil's name) but to mend and repair after your arse?—Good words, friend, said the bee (having now pruned himself, and being disposed to droll): I'll give you my hand and word to come near your kennel no more; I was never in such a confounded pickle since I was born.—Sirrah. replied the spider. if it were not for breaking an old custom in our family, never to stir abroad against an enemy. I should come and teach you better manners.—I pray have patience, said the bee, or you'll spend your substance. and. for aught 1 see, you may stand in need of it all, toward the repair of your house.—Rogue, rogue. replied the spider. yet methinks you should have more respect to a person whom all the world allows to be so much your betters. By my troth, said the bee, the comparison will amount to a very good jest: and you will do me a favour to let me know the reasons that all the world is pleased to use in so hopeful a dispute. At this the spider, having swelled himself into the size and posture of a disputant. began his argument in the true spirit of controversy, with resolution to be heartily scurrilous and angry to urge on his own reasons, without the least regard to the answers or objections of his opposite; and fully predetermined in his mind against all conviction.

Not to disparage myself. said he. by the comparison with such a rascal, what art thou but a vagabond without house or home, without stock or inheritance? born to no possession of your own, but a pair of wings and a drone-pipe. Your livelihood is a universal plunder upon nature; a freebooter over fields and gardens; and, for the sake of stealing will rob a nettle as easily as a violet. Whereas I am a domestic animal, furnished with a native stock within myself. This large castle (to show my improvements in the mathematics) is all built with my own hands, and the materials extracted altogether out of my own person.

I am glad, answered the bee, to hear you grant at least that I am come honestly by my wings and my voice; for then, it seems, I am obliged to Heaven alone for my flights and my music; and Providence would never have bestowed on me two such gifts. without designing them for the noblest ends. I visit indeed all the flowers and blossoms of the field and garden; but whatever I collect thence enriches myself, without the least injury to their beauty. their smell. or their taste. Now, for you and your skill in architecture and other mathematics. I have little to say: in that building of yours there might, for aught I know, have been labour and method enough; but. by woeful experience for us both, it is too plain the materials are naught; and I hope you will henceforth take warning, and consider duration and matter, as well as method and art. You boast indeed of being obliged to no other creature, but of drawing and spinning out all from yourself; that is to say, if we may judge of the liquor in the vessel by what issues out, you possess a good plentiful store of dirt and poison in your breast; and, though I would by no means lessen or disparage your genuine stock of either, yet I doubt you are somewhat obliged, for an increase of both. to a little foreign assistance. Your inherent portion of dirt does not fail of acquisitions, by sweepings exhaled from below: and one insect furnishes you with a share of poison to destroy another. So that. in short. the question comes all to this; whether is the nobler being of the two, that which, by a lazy contemplation of four inches round, by an overweening pride, feeding and engendering on itself, turns all into excrement and venom, producing nothing at all but flybane and a cobweb; or that which, by a universal range, with long search, much study, true judgment, and distinction of things, brings home honey and wax.

This dispute was managed with such eagerness, clamour, and warmth, that the two parties of books, in arms below, stood silent a while, waiting in suspense what would be the issue; which was not long undetermined; for the bee, grown impatient at so much loss of time, fled straight away to a bed of roses, without looking for a reply. and left the spider, like an orator, collected in himself, and just prepared to burst out.

It happened upon this emergency that Æsop broke silence first. He had been of late most barbarously treated by a strange effect of the regent's humanity, who had torn off his title-page, sorely defaced one half of his leaves, and chained him fast among a shelf of moderns. Where, soon discovering how high the quarrel was likely to proceed, he tried all his arts, and turned himself to a thousand forms. At length, in the borrowed shape of an ass, the regent mistook him for a modern; by which means he had time and opportunity to escape to the ancients, just when the spider and the bee were entering into their contest; to which he gave his attention with a world of pleasure, and when it was ended, swore in the loudest key that in all his life he had never known two cases so parallel and adapt to each other as that in the window and this upon the shelves. The disputants, said he, have admirably managed the dispute between them, have taken in the full strength of all that is to be said on both sides, and exhausted the substance of every argument *pro* and *con*. It is but to adjust the reasonings of both to the present quarrel, then to compare and apply the labours and fruits of each, as the bee has learnedly deduced them. and we shall find the conclusion fall plain and close upon the moderns and us. For pray, gentlemen, was ever anything so modern as the spider in his air, his turns, and his paradoxes? he argues in the behalf of you, his brethren, and himself with many boastings of his native stock and great genius; that he spins and spits wholly from himself, and scorns to own any obligation or assistance from without. Then he displays to you his great skill in architecture and improvement in the mathematics. To all this the bee, as an advocate retained by us the ancients, thinks fit to answer, that, if one may judge of the great genius or inventions of the moderns by what they have produced, you will hardly have countenance to bear you out in boasting of either. Erect your schemes with as much method and skill as you please; yet, if the materials be nothing but dirt, spun out of your own entrails (the guts of modern brains), the edifice will conclude at last in a cobweb; the duration of which, like that of other spiders' webs, may be imputed to their being forgotten, or neglected, or hid in a corner. For anything else of genuine that the moderns may pretend to, I cannot recollect; unless it be a large vein of wrangling and satire, much of a nature and substance with the spider's poison; which, however, they pretend to spit wholly out of themselves, is improved by the same arts, by feeding upon the insects and vermin of the age. As for us the ancients, we are content with the bee, to pretend to nothing of our own beyond our wings and our voice: that is to say, our flights and our language. For the rest, whatever we have got has been by infinite labour and search, and ranging through every corner of nature; the difference is, that, instead of dirt and poison. we have rather chosen to fill our hives with honey and wax; thus furnishing mankind with the two noblest of things, which are sweetness and light.

It is wonderful to conceive the tumult arisen among the books upon the close of this long descant of Æsop: both parties took the hint, and heightened their animosities so on a sudden. that they resolved it should come to a battle. Immediately the two main bodies withdrew, under their several ensigns. to the farther parts of the library, and there entered into cabals and consults upon the present emergency. The moderns were in very warm debates upon the choice of their leaders; and nothing less than the fear impending from their enemies could have kept them from mutinies upon this occasion. The difference was greatest among the horse, where every, private trooper pretended to the chief command, from Tasso and Milton to Dryden and Withers. The light-horse were commanded by Cowley and Despréaux. There came the bowmen under their valiant leaders, Des Cartes, Gassendi. and Hobbes; whose strength was such that they could shoot their arrows beyond the atmosphere, never to fall down again, but turn like that of Evander, into meteors; or, like the cannon-ball, into stars. Paracelsus brought a squadron of stinkpot-flingers from the snowy mountains of Rhætia. There came a vast body of dragoons, of different nations, under the leading of Harvey* their great aga: part armed with scythes, the weapons of death; part with lances and long knives, all steeped in poison; part shot bullets of a most malignant nature, and used white powder, which infallibly killed without report. There came several bodies of heavy-armed foot, all mercenaries, under the ensigns of Guicciardini, Davila, Polydore, Virgil, Buchanan, Mariana, Camden, and others. The engineers were commanded by Regiomontanus and Wilkins. The rest was a confused multitude, led by Scotus, Aquinas, and Bellarmine; of mighty bulk and stature, but without either arms, courage, or discipline. In the last place came infinite swarms of calones. a disorderly rout led by L'Estrange; rogues and ragamuffins, that follow the camp for nothing but the plunder, all without coats to cover them.

* Discoverer of the circulation of the blood.

The army of the ancients was much fewer in number: Homer led the horse, and Pindar the light-horse; Euclid was chief engineer; Plato and Aristotle commanded the bowmen; Herodotus and Livy the foot; Hippocrates the dragoons; the allies. led by Vossius and Temple, brought up the rear.

All things violently tending to a decisive battle, Fame, who much frequented, and had a large apartment formerly assigned her in the regal library, fled up straight to Jupiter, to whom she delivered a faithful account of all that passed between the two parties below; for among the gods she always tells truth. Jove, in great concern, convokes a council in the milky way. The senate assembled, he declares the occasion of convening them: a bloody battle just impendent between two mighty armies of ancient and modern creatures, called books, wherein the celestial interest was but too deeply concerned. Momus, the patron of the moderns, made an excellent speech in their favour, which was answered by Pallas, the protectress of the ancients. The assembly was divided in their affections; when Jupiter commanded the book of fate to be laid before him. Immediately were brought by Mercury three large volumes in folio, containing memoirs of all things past, present, and to come. The clasps were of silver double gilt, the cover sof celestial turkey leather, and the paper such as here on earth might pass almost for vellum. Jupiter, having silently read the decree, would communicate the import to none, but presently shut up the book.

Without the doors of this assembly there attended a vast number of light, nimble gods, menial servants to Jupiter: these are his ministering instruments in all affairs below. They travel in a caravan, more or less together, and are fastened to each other, like a link of galley-slaves, by a light chain, which passes from them to Jupiter's great toe: and yet, in receiving or delivering a message, they may never approach above the lowest step of his throne, where he and they whisper to each other through a large hollow trunk. These deities are called by mortal men accidents or events; but the gods call them second causes. Jupiter having delivered his message to a certain number of these divinities, they flew immediately down to the pinnacle of the regal library, and consulting a few minutes, entered unseen, and disposed the parties according to their orders.

Meanwhile Momus, fearing the worst, and calling to mind an ancient prophecy which bore no very good face to his children the moderns, bent his flight to the region of a malignant deity called Criticism. She dwelt on the top of a snowy mountain in Nova Zembla; there Momus found her extended in her den, upon the spoils of numberless volumes, half devoured. At her right hand sat Ignorance, her father and husband, blind with age; at her left, Pride, her mother, dressing her up in the scraps of paper herself had torn. There was opinion, her sister, light of foot, hoodwinked, and headstrong, yet giddy and perpetually turning. About her played her children, Noise and Impudence, Dulness and Vanity, Positiveness, Pedantry, and Ill-manners. The goddess herself had claws like a cat; her head, and ears, and voice, resembled those of an ass; her teeth fallen out before, her eyes turned inward, as if she looked only upon herself; her diet was the overflowing of her own gall; her spleen was so large as to stand prominent, like a dug of the first rate; nor wanted excrescencies in form of teats, at which a crew of ugly monsters were greedily sucking; and, what is wonderful to conceive, the bulk of spleen increased faster than the sucking could diminish it. Goddess, said Momus, can you sit idly here while our devout worshippers, the moderns, are this minute entering into a cruel battle, and perhaps now lying under the swords of their enemies? who then hereafter will ever sacrifice or build altars to our divinities? Haste, therefore, to the British isle, and, if possible, prevent their destruction; while I make factions among the gods, and gain them over to our party.

Momus, having thus delivered himself, staid not for an answer, but left the goddess to her own resentment. Up she rose in a rage, and, as it is the form upon such occasions, began a soliloquy: It is I (said she) who gave wisdom to infants and idiots; by me children grew wiser than their parents, by me beaux become politicians, and school-boys judges of philosophy: by me sophisters debate and conclude upon the depths of knowledge; and coffee-house wits, instinct by me, can correct an author's style, and display his minutest errors without understanding a syllable of his matter or his language; by me striplings spend their judgment, as they do their estate, before it comes into their hands. It is I who have deposed wit and kowledge from their empire over poetry, and advanced myself in their stead. And shall a few upstart ancients dare to oppose me?—But come, my aged parent, and you my children dear, and thou. my beauteous sister; let us ascend my chariot, and haste to assist our devout moderns, who are now sacrificing to us a hecatomb, as I perceive by that grateful smell which from thence reaches my nostrils.

The goddess and her train, having mounted the chariot. which was drawn by tame geese. flew over infinite regions shedding her influence in due places, till at length she arrived at her beloved island of Britain; but in hovering over its metropolis, what blessings did she not let fall upon her seminaries of Gresham and Covent-garden! And now she reached the fatal plain of St. James's library, at what time the two armies were upon the point to engage: where, entering with all her caravan unseen, and landing upon a case of shelves, now desert, but once inhabited by a colony of virtuosos, she staid a while to observe the posture of both armies.

But here the tender cares of a mother began to fill her thoughts and move in her breast: for at the head of a troop of modern bowmen she cast her eyes upon her son Wotton, to whom the fates had assigned a very short thread. Wotton, a young hero, whom an unknown father of mortal race begot by stolen embraces with this goddess. He was the darling of his mother above all her children, and she resolved to go and comfort him. But first, according to the good old custom of deities, she cast about to change her shape, for fear the divinity of her countenance might dazzle his mortal sight and overcharge the rest of his senses. She therefore gathered up her person into an octavo compass: her body grew white and arid, and split in pieces with dryness; the thick turned into pasteboard, and the thin into paper; upon which her parents and children artfully strewed a black juice, or decoction of gall and soot. in form of letters: her head, and voice, and spleen, kept their primitive form; and that which before was a cover of skin did still continue so. In this guise she marched on towards the moderns, undistinguishable in shape and dress from the divine Bentley, Wotton's dearest friend. Brave Wotton, said the goddess, why do our troops stand idle here, to spend their present vigour and opportunity of the day? away, let us haste to the generals, and advise to give the onset immediately. Having spoken thus, she took the ugliest of her monsters, full glutted from her spleen, and flung it invisibly into his mouth, wich, flying straight up into his head, squeezed out his eye-balls, gave him a distorted look, and half over-turned his brain. Then she privately ordered two of her beloved children, Dulness, and Ill-manners. closely to attend his person in all encounters. Having thus accoutred him, she vanished in a mist, and the hero perceived it was the goddess his mother.

The destined hour of fate being now arrived. the fight began; whereof, before I dare adventure to make a particular description, I must, after the example of other authors, petition for a hundred tongues, and mouths. and hands. and pens, which would all be too little to perform so immense a work. Say. goddess. that presidest over history. who it was that first advanced in the field of battle! Paracelsus, at the head of his dragoons, observing Galen in the adverse wing, darted his javelin with a mighty force, which the brave ancient received upon his shield, the point, breaking in the second fold.

. . . . *Hic pauca*
. . . . *desunt.*

They bore the wounded aga on their shields to his chariot . . . .

Desunt . . . .
nonnulla. . . . .

Then Aristotle, observing Bacon advance with a furious mien, drew his bow to the head, and let fly his arrow, which missed the valiant modern and went whizzing over his head; but Des Cartes it hit; the steel point quickly found a defect in his headpiece; it pierced the leather and the pasteboard, and went in at his right eye. The torture of the pain whirled the valiant bowman round till death, like a star of superior influence, drew him into his own vortex . . . .

Ingens hiatus. . . . .
hic in MS. . . . .

. . . . .when Homer appeared at the head of the cavalry, mounted on a furious horse, with difficulty managed by the rider himself, but which no other mortal durst approach; he rode among the enemy's ranks, and bore down all before him. Say goddess, whom he slew first and whom he slew last! First, Gondibert advanced against him, clad in heavy armour and mounted on a staid, sober gelding, not so famed for his speed as his docility in kneeling whenever his rider would mount or alight. He had made a vow to Pallas that he would never leave the field till he had spoiled Homer of his armour: madman, who had never once seen the wearer, nor understood his strength! Him Homer overthrew, horse and man, to the ground, there to be trampled

174

and choked in the dirt. Then with a long spear he slew Denham, a stout modern, who from his father's side derived his lineage from Apollo, but his mother, was of mortal race. He fell, and bit the earth. The celestial part Apollo took, and made it a star; but the terrestrial lay wallowing upon the ground. Then Homer slew Sam Wesley with a kick of his horse's heel; he took Perrault by mighty force out of his saddle, then hurled him at Fontenelle, with the same blow dashing out both their brains.

On the left wing of the horse Virgil appeared, in shining armour, completely fitted to his body: he was mounted on a dapple-grey steed, the slowness of whose pace was an effect of the highest mettle and vigour. He cast his eye on the adverse wing, with a desire to find an object worthy of his valour, when behold upon a sorrel gelding of a monstrous size appeared a foe, issuing from among the thickest of the enemy's squadrons; but his speed was less than his noise; for his horse, old and lean, spent the dregs of his strength in a high trot, which, though it made slow advances, yet caused a loud clashing of his armour terrible to hear. The two cavaliers had now approached within the throw of a lance, when the stranger desired a parley, and lifting up the vizor of his helmet, a face hardly appeared from within which, after a pause, was known for that of the renowned Dryden. The brave ancient suddenly started, as one possessed with surprise and disappointment together; for the helmet was nine times too large for the head, which appeared situate far in the hinder part, even like the lady in a lobster, or like a mouse under a canopy of state, or like a shrivelled beau from within the penthouse of a modern periwig; and the voice was suited to the visage, sounding weak and remote. Dryden, in a long harangue, soothed up the good ancient; called him father, and, by a large deduction of genealogies, made it plainly appear that they were nearly related. Then he humbly proposed an exchange of armour, as a lasting mark of hospitality between them. Virgil consented (for the goddess Diffidence came unseen, and cast a mist, before his eyes), though his was of gold and cost a hundred beeves, the other's but of rusty iron. However, this glittering armour became the modern yet worse than his own. Then they agreed to exchange horses; but, when it came to the trial, Dryden was afraid and utterly unable to mount.

. . . . *Alter hiatus*
. . . . *in MS.*

Lucan appeared upon a fiery horse of admirable shape, but headstrong, bearing the rider where he list over the field; he made a mighty slaughter among the enemy's horse; which destruction to stop, Blackmore, a famous modern (but one of the mercenaries), strenuously opposed himself, and darted his javelin with a strong hand, which, falling short of its mark, struck deep in the earth. Then Lucan threw a lance; but Æsculapius came unseen and turned off the point. Brave modern, said Lucan, I perceive some god protects you, for never did my arm so deceive me before: but what mortal can contend with a god? Therefore, let us fight no longer, but present gifts to each other. Lucan then bestowed the modern a pair of spurs, and Blackmore gave Lucan a bridle.

Pauca desunt. . . . .

Creech: but the goddess Dulness took a cloud, formed into the shape of Horace, armed and mounted, and placed in a flying posture before him. Glad was the cavalier to begin a combat with a flying foe, and pursued the image, threatening aloud; till at last it led to the peaceful bower of his father, Ogleby, by whom he was disarmed and assigned to his repose.

Then Pindar slew ——, and ——, and Oldham, and ——, and Afra* the Amazon, light of foot; never advancing in a direct line, but wheeling with

* Mrs. Afra Behn.

incredible agility and force, he made a terrible slaughter among the enemy's light horse. Him, when Cowley observed, his generous heart burnt within him, and he advanced against the fierce ancient, imitating his address, his pace, and career, as well as the vigour of his horse and his own skill would allow. When the two cavaliers had approached within the length of three javelins, first Cowley threw a lance, which missed Pindar, and, passing into the enemy's ranks, fell ineffectual to the ground. Then Pindar darted a javelin so large and weighty, that scarce a dozen cavaliers as cavaliers are in our degenerate days, could raise it from the ground; yet he threw it with ease, and it went, by an unerring hand, singing through the air; nor could the modern have avoided present death if he had not luckily opposed the shield that had been given him by Venus.* And now both heroes drew their swords; but the modern was so aghast and disordered that he knew not where he was; his shield dropped from his hands; thrice he fled, and thrice he could not escape; at last he turned, and lifting up his hand in the posture of a suppliant, Godlike Pindar, said he, spare my life, and posses my horse, with these arms, beside the ransom which my friends will give when they hear I am alive and your prisoner. Dog! said Pindar, let your ransom stay with your friends; but your carcase shall be left for the fowls of the air and the beasts of the field. With that he raised his sword, and, with a mighty stroke, cleft the wretched modern in twain, the sword pursuing the blow; and one half lay panting on the ground, to be trod in pieces by the horses' feet; the other half was borne by the frighted steed through the field. This Venus took, washed it seven times in ambrosia, then struck it thrice with a sprig of amaranth; upon which the leather grew round and soft, and the leaves turned into feathers, and, being gilded before, continued gilded

* His poem called *The Mistress*.

still; so it became a dove, and she harnessed it to
her chariot . . . .
. . .   . *Hiatus valde de-*
. . . . *flendus in MS.*

The episode of Bentley and Wotton.

Day being far spent, and the numerous forces
of the moderns half inclining to a retreat, there issued
forth from a squadron of their heavy-armed foot a
captain whose name was Bentley, the most deformed
of all the moderns; tall, but without shape or come-
liness; large, but without strength or proportion.
His armour was patched up of a thousand incoherent
pieces; and the sound of it, as he marched, was loud
and dry, like that made by the fall of a sheet of lead,
which an Etesian wind blows suddenly down from
the roof of some steeple. His helmet was of old rusty
iron, but the vizor was brass, which, tainted by his
breath, corrupted into copperas, nor wanted gall
from the same fountain; so that, whenever provoked
by anger or labour, an atramentous quality, of most
malignant nature, was seen to distil from his lips.
In his right hand he grasped a flail, and (that he might
never be unprovided of an offensive weapon) a
vessel full of ordure in his left. Thus completely armed,
he advanced with a slow and heavy pace where the
modern chiefs were holding a consult upon the sum
of things; who, as he came onwards, laughed to behold
his crooked leg and humped shoulder, which his boot
and armour, vainly endeavouring to hide, were
forced to comply with and expose. The generals
made use of him for his talent of railing; which
kept within government, proved frequently of great
service to their cause, but, at other times, did more
mischief than good; for, at the least touch of offence,
and often without any at all, he would, like a wounded
elephant, convert it against his leaders. Such, at
this juncture, was the disposition of Bentley; grieved
to see the enemy prevail, and dissatisfied with every-

body's conduct but his own. he humbly gave the modern generals to understand that he conceived, with great submission, they were all a pack of rogues, and fools, and sons of whores, and d—d cowards, and confounded loggerheads, and illiterate whelps, and nonsensical scoundrels; that, if himself had been constituted general, those presumptuous dogs, the ancients, would long before this have been beaten out of the field. You, said he, sit here idle; but when I, or any other valiant modern, kill an enemy, you are sure to seize the spoil. But I will not march one foot against the foe till you all swear to me that whomever I take or kill, his arms I shall quietly possess. Bentley having spoken thus, Scaliger, bestowing him a sour look. Miscreant prater! said he, eloquent only in thine own eyes, thou railest without wit, or truth, or discretion. The malignity of thy temper perverteth nature; thy learning makes thee more barbarous; thy study of humanity more inhuman; thy converse among poets more grovelling, miry, and dull. All arts of civilising others render thee rude and untractable; courts have taught thee ill manners, and polite conversation has finished thee a pedant. Besides. a greater coward burdeneth not the army. But never despond; I pass my word, whatever spoil thou takest shall certainly be thy own; though I hope that vile carcase will first become a prey to kites and worms.

Bentley durst not reply; but, half choked with spleen and rage, withdrew, in full resolution of performing some great achievement. With him, for his aid and companion, he took his beloved Wotton; resolving by policy or surprise to attempt some neglected quarter of the ancient's army. They began their march over carcases of their slaughtered friends; then to the right of their own forces; then wheeled northward, till they came to Aldrovandus's tomb, which they passed on the side of the declining sun. And now they arrived, with fear, toward the enemy's outguards; looking about. if haply they might spy the quarters of the wounded, or some straggling

12*

sleepers, unarmed and remote from the rest. As when two mongrel curs, whom native greediness and domestic want provoke and join in partnership, though fearful, nightly to invade the folds of some rich grazier, they, with tails depressed and lolling tongues, creep soft and slow; meanwhile the conscious moon, now in her zenith, on their guilty heads darts perpendicular rays; nor dare they bark, though much provoked at her refulgent visage, whether seen in puddle by reflection or in sphere direct; but one surveys the region round, while the other scouts the plain, if haply to discover, at distance from the flock, some carcase half devoured, the refuse of gorged wolves or ominous ravens. So marched this lovely, loving pair of friends, nor with less fear and circumspection, when at a distance they might perceive two shining suits of armour hanging upon an oak, and the owners not far off in a profound sleep. The two friends drew lots, and the pursuing of this adventure fell to Bentley; on he went, and in his van Confusion and Amaze, while Horror and Affright brought up the rear. As he came near, behold two heroes of the ancient's army, Phalaris and Æsop, lay fast asleep; Bentley would fain have despatched them both, and, stealing close, aimed his flail at Phalaris's breast. But then the goddess Affright, interposing, caught the modern in her icy arms, and dragged him from the danger she foresaw; both the dormant heroes happened to turn at the same instant, though soundly sleeping, and busy in a dream. For Phalaris was just that minute dreaming how a most vile poetaster had lampooned him, and how he had got him roaring in his bull. And Æsop dreamed that, as he and the ancient chiefs were lying on the ground, a wild ass broke loose, ran about, trampling and kicking and dunging in their faces. Bentley, leaving the two heroes asleep, seized on both their armours, and withdrew in quest of his darling Wotton.

He, in the meantime, had wandered long in search of some enterprise, till at length he arrived at a small

180

rivulet that issued from a fountain hard by, called, in the language of mortal men, Helicon. Here he stopped, and, parched with thirst, resolved to allay it in this limpid stream. Thrice with profane hands he essayed to raise the water to his lips, and thrice it slipped all through his fingers. Then he stooped prone on his breast, but, ere his mouth had kissed the liquid crystal, Apollo came, and in the channel held his shield betwixt the modern and the fountain, so that he drew up nothing but mud. For, although no fountain on earth can compare with the clearness of Helicon, yet there lies at bottom a thick sediment of slime and mud; for so Apollo begged of Jupiter, as a punishment to those who durst attempt to taste it with unhallowed lips, and for a lesson to all not to draw too deep or far from the spring.

At the fountain-head Wotton discerned two heroes; the one he could not distinguish, but the other was soon known for Temple, general of the allies to the ancients. His back was turned, and he was employed in drinking large draughts in his helmet from the fountain, where he had withdrawn himself to rest from the toils of the war. Wotton, observing him, with quaking knees and trembling hands, spoke thus to himself: O that I could kill this destroyer of our army, what renown should I purchase among the chiefs! but to issue out against him, man against man, shield against shield, and lance against lance, what modern of us dare? for he fights like a god, and Pallas or Apollo are ever at his elbow. But, O mother! if what Fame reports be true, that I am the son of so great a goddess, grant me to hit Temple with this lance, that the stroke may send him to hell, and that I may return in safety and triumph, laden with his spoils. The first part of this prayer the gods granted at the intercession of his mother and of Momus; but the rest, by a perverse wind sent from Fate, was scattered in the air. Then Wotton grasped his lance, and, brandishing it thrice over his head, darted it with all his might; the goddess, his mother,

at the same time adding strength to his arm. Away
the lance went hizzing, and reached even to the belt
of the averted ancient, upon which lightly grazing,
it fell to the ground. Temple neither felt the weapon
touch him nor heard it fall: and Wotton might
have escaped to his army, with the honour of having
remitted his lance against so great a leader un-
revenged; but Apollo, enraged that a javelin flung by
the assistance of so foul a goddess should pollute
his fountain, put on the shape of ——, and softly
came to young Boyle, who then accompanied Temple:
he pointed first to the lance, then to the distant
modern that flung it, and commanded the young
hero to take immediate revenge. Boyle, clad in a suit
of armour which had been given him by all the gods,
immediately advenced against the trembling foe, who
now fled before him. As a young lion in the Libyan
plains, or Araby desert, sent by his aged sire to hunt
for prey, or health, or exercise, he scours along,
wishing to meet some tiger from the mountains, or a
furious boar; if chance a wild ass, with brayings
importune, affronts his ear, the generous beast,
though loathing to distain his claws with blood so
vile, much yet, provoked at the offensive noise, which
Echo, foolish nymph, like her ill-judging sex, repeats
much louder, and with more delight than Philomela's
song, he vindicates the honour of the forest, and hunts
the noisy long-eared animal. So Wotton fled, so
Boyle pursued. But Wotton, heavy armed and slow
of foot, began to slack his course, when his lover
Bentley appeared, returning laden with the spoils
of the two sleeping ancients. Boyle observed him
well and soon discovering the helmet and shield of
Phalaris his friend, both which he had lately with
his own hands new polished and gilt, rage sparkled
in his eyes, and, leaving his pursuit after Wotton,
he furiously rushed on against this new approacher.
Fain would he be revenged on both; but both now
fled different ways: and, as a woman in a little house
that gets a painful livelihood by spinning, if chance her

geese be scattered o'er the common. she courses round the plain from side to side, compelling here and there the stragglers to the flock; they cackle loud, and flutter o'er the champaign; so Boyle pursued. so fled this pair of friends: finding at length their flight was vain, they bravely joined, and drew themselves in phalanx. First Bentley threw a spear with all his force, hoping to pierce the enemy's breast; but Pallas came unseen. and in the air took off the point, and clapped on one of lead, which, after a dead bang against the enemy's shield. fell blunted to the ground. Then Boyle, observing well his time, took up a lance of wondrous length and sharpness; and, as this pair of friends compacted, stood close side to side, he wheeled him to the right, and, with unusual force, darted the weapon. Bentley saw his fate approach, and flanking, down his arms close to his ribs, hoping to save his body, in went the point, passing through arm and side. nor stopped or spent its force till it had also pierced the valiant Wotton, who. going to sustain his dying friend, shared his fate. As when a skilful cook has trussed a brace of woodcocks, he with iron skewer pierces the tender sides of both, their legs and wings close pinioned to the ribs; so was this pair of friends transfixed, till down they fell, joined in their lives, joined in their deaths; so closely joined that Charon would mistake them both for one, and waft them over Styx for half his fare. Farewell, beloved, loving pair; few equals have you left behind: and happy and immortal shall you be, if all my wit and eloquence can make you.

And now . . . .
Desunt cœtera.

183

This is the end of this publication.

Any remaining blank pages are for our book binding requirements and are blank on purpose.

To search thousands of interesting publications like this one, please remember to visit our website at:

http://www.kessinger.net

CPSIA information can be obtained at www.ICGtesting.com
Printed in the USA
BVOW04*2253070615

403552BV00003BB/21/P